A POSTCARD FROM
CARDIFF

BRIAN LEE & AMANDA HARVEY

D1555782

The History Press

In memory of Patricia Isabel Collins

(30 August 1923 – 11 August 2010)

A true Cardiffian

Ladies of the Court
From Tiger Bay and
Mary Ann Street, Cardiff

First published 2011

The History Press
The Mill, Brimscombe Port
Stroud, Gloucestershire, GL5 2QG
www.thehistorypress.co.uk

© Brian Lee and Amanda Harvey, 2011

The right of Brian Lee and Amanda Harvey to be identified as the
Authors of this work has been asserted in accordance with the
Copyrights, Designs and Patents Act 1988.

British Library Cataloguing in Publication Data.
A catalogue record for this book is available from the British Library.

ISBN 978 0 7524 5836 6

Typesetting and origination by The History Press
Printed in Great Britain

Contents

Foreword

It was once said that nostalgia 'is a thing of the past'! However, since my schoolboy days (and they were many moons ago), my love for all things old, in my beloved Cardiff, is still fresh in my mind. There were several reasons, it seemed to me, to get to know your town or city.

In my case, I was a schoolboy during Second World War, and at the same time, 1939 to be precise, my homelife was devastated when my father died suddenly, at the age of thirty-eight; I was just six years old. My three brothers were also still only of school age, and all attended Gladstone Boys' School, in Cathays. A great responsibility fell upon my mother's shoulders and she made the best of a bad job in clothing, feeding and devoting her life to looking after us as she thought fit, until her untimely death at the age of fifty.

My interest in building up collections, such as stamps, cigarette cards, badges was easily obtained. I even managed to get a collection of US Army uniform/cap badges, when the 'Yanks' were stationed in Maindy Barracks, Heath Park and Whitchurch Common, prior to D-Day. As well as gum and candy, it was badges of their units like the 'Screaming Eagles', and the empty cigarette packets: 'Lucky Strike', 'Camel', and 'Chesterfield'. All these items were currency to a young schoolboy at that time, but one thing we saw little of – photographs. They had almost disappeared due to the shortage of cameras and I seem to remember that you needed a licence to own a camera during wartime.

Now that I am in my seventies, my passion is old photographs of years gone by, and in particular those relating to Cardiff. Some twenty years ago, I joined a postcard collecting club and was amazed at the number of old topographical postcards of Cardiff which existed, along with many other cities, towns and villages, so I was off to collector's fairs around the country in my search for old cards.

I have seen so many changes in my lifetime, particularly in the city centre, and with the aid of my collection, I still enjoy seeing different views of Queen Street (before pedestrianisation), St Mary Street, and popular shop fronts, as well as civic buildings and parks. Just look above the shop fronts in the city centre and you will see wonderful Victorian architecture, such as the Indoor Market and the Philharmonic Hotel in St Mary Street. Sadly, Queen Street is rapidly losing its identity, where glass structures seem to be sprouting up and replacing some unique buildings. For instance, the old cinemas: every child's dream was created by the films of the period – such as Tarzan's adventures, pre-John Wayne Westerns, and war films, staying in our minds for years.

Brian and Amanda have captured the essence of the meaning of true nostalgia, which I am sure readers will spend many a happy hour discussing with family and friends; the history of such-and-such a street, shop or church etc long gone, but the postcards and images depicted in *A Postcard From Cardiff* will stay for ever.

At the South Wales Postcard Club, we meet every month in Cardiff and enjoy club members' various interests in old postcards, ephemera and help with research on family history, etc. We also have speakers to give talks on postcard subjects, often about one's particular town or city. Our club is open to all members of the public with like-minded interests.

I feel that as I am now so much part of Cardiff's fabric, it is with great interest and delight that publications with local interest by Brian Lee's numerous editions that I am still learning about my beloved Cardiff.

Alun Williams, 2011

Introduction

The beauty of collecting picture postcards is that you can choose your own subject – be it teddy bears or trolley buses.

The first picture postcards in this country appeared around 1894, but it wasn't until 1902 that the hobby really became popular. Because of printing costs, many of the picture postcards were printed in Germany, but all that changed with the coming of the First World War.

You only have to look at the messages written on the reverse side of some of the early picture postcards to see that they were ideal for sending notes to family and friends, in the days when one could rely on the mail arriving the next day.

They often give us a nostalgic peep into the past, like the one I have before me now, number seven in the National Pageant Of Wales series (the pageant was held in Sophia Gardens, Cardiff, in 1909). It is addressed to Mr T. Ronicle, No. 4 Jubilee Street, Burnham, Somerset, and was posted on 3 August 1909. It reads:

> Dear Tom, have just arrived home, after having an enjoyable day. Mother and Dad hope you are all enjoying yourselves and having nice weather. Remember me to Gertie. Yours truly, Nellie.

It has been estimated that there are around 500 picture-postcard dealers in this country alone and more than 20,000 serious collectors. Then there are the not-too-serious collectors like myself, whose real interest is in a particular subject.

In my case, picture postcards of old Cardiff; incidentally some of the ones I have were published by the *Western Mail*. There are also around twenty auction houses which specialise in picture postcards and some seventy picture-postcard collectors' clubs.

Picture-postcard collectors travel to the various postcard fairs that are held throughout the year. One of the biggest is the Bloomsbury one in London, and every month there are around 120 stands. Collectors even have their own magazine, *Picture Postcard Monthly* (see their website: www.postcard.co.uk/ppm).

The days when you could buy picture postcards for a few pence are long gone. Some street and shop scenes fetch around £20 or more. Yet others – of say Cardiff's civic centre buildings – can be bought for just a pound or two. I bought several of the equestrian statue of the 1st Viscount Lord Tredegar – mounted on his favourite charger, Sir Briggs, outside Cardiff's City Hall – by Raphael Tuck & Sons, The Strand Series, and the Royal Photographical Company, for just a few pounds.

But if you should come across a picture postcard of a suffragette, it will probably set you back between £400-£500. An unused and rather grubby picture postcard of the *Titanic*, brought off the ship by survivor Edith Brown and bearing a message to her step-sister, was sold at Sotherbys in 1998 for £14,375!

We have Cardiff-born photographer Ernest Thomas Bush, who in 1924 set up his own picture-publishing company, the Bush Photographic Company, to thank for documenting South Wales's past. However, his photographs had been appearing on picture postcards as early as 1901.

The period between 1901-1909 really set the standard for the picture-postcard collectors of today and is known as the Golden Age. Most middle-class families could boast an album and postcard collecting became a worldwide craze. In this country they cost a half-penny to buy and the same amount to send.

Ever since, picture postcards have continued to depict our history, social or otherwise; they have featured sportsmen and women, actors and actresses, politicians, disasters, exhibitions, towns and villages, shipping and transport. The modern picture postcards of today, by contrast, feature pop music, glamour and celebrities, among the many subjects available.

You name it and there is probably a picture postcard depicting it. Second only to stamp collecting as a hobby, old and contemporary picture postcards are eagerly sought after.

Brian Lee, 2011

1

Cardiff Castle

Cardiff Castle was built on the foundations of a Roman fort and parts of the original Roman wall can be seen in Castle Street, south of the castle. In 1947, John Crichton-Stuart, Marquis of Bute, presented to the citizens of Cardiff the castle as an outright gift, for their use and enjoyment in perpetuity.

Cardiff Castle.

A scene depicting the frontage of Cardiff Castle. Horse-drawn trams were still around, but the stone animals adorning the Castle wall and railings had not yet been installed. Only a lion can be seen next to the gate on the right.

From *Cardiff Castle: Its History and Architecture* by John P. Grant:

> It is thought by some authorities that the mound upon which The Keep stands is the work of the Danes who had a strong settlement in the district during the tenth and eleventh centuries, but it is more probable that the moated mound was raised after the Norman Conquest, as these mounds were, in fact, the castles with which the Conqueror secured the possession of his territory.
>
> (The Royal Photographic Company, London)

In 1883, Lord Bute gave orders that the wall in front of the castle should be mounted with animal figures; however it wasn't until 1888 that his instructions were finally completed. This card is from around 1905. (Photochrom Co. Ltd)

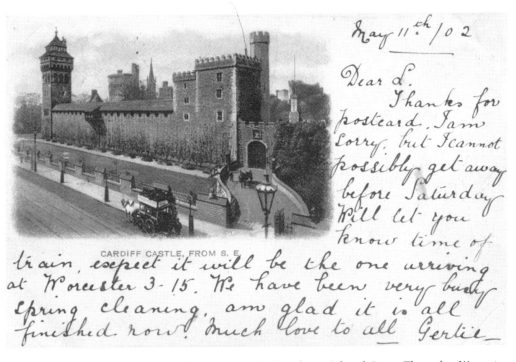

This unidentified postcard of the castle was sent to Mrs Baynham, Calgarth Lawn, Thorneloe, Worcester on 11 May 1902. (Postcard publisher unidentified)

From *A History of the City* by William Rees:

> The original lions were deemed to be too modest in demeanour, savouring as pets than of roaring lions and were later returned for re-touching.

The animals were moved to their present site in 1928 when a vulture, leopard, pelican, raccoons and an ant-eater were added – along with a bear, which had replaced the original polar bear. (Raphael Tuck & Sons, posted in 1904)

From *Cardiff Castle: Its History and Architecture* by John P. Grant:

The south wall was rebuilt between 1865 and 1870 by the 3rd Marquis of Bute and his architect, William Burgess, who restored the whole of the face work.

The fifteenth-century Octagon Tower, crowned with a spire at the north-west corner of the new Great Hall. (Judges Ltd, Hastings)

The Marquis of Bute appointed the great architect William Burgess to carry out the reconstruction of the castle. To the left of the picture can be seen the famous clock tower. (Grosvenor Series)

Trams were in vogue when Ernest T. Bush took this rare postcard picture of Duke Street and Cardiff Castle in around 1904. (The Bush Photographic Company, Cardiff)

The magnificent Clock Tower, built between 1867-72, contains a complete suite of apartments. (Valentine & Sons Ltd)

From *Cardiff Castle: Its History and Architecture* by John P. Grant:

The chimney-piece depicts the summer amusement of lovers. It bears the legend *AESTATE VIRESCO* which translates 'In summer I grow green', perhaps with the suggestion that summer renews our youth.

(Valentine & Sons Ltd)

The Castle Lodge, in North Road, was the lock house for the Glamorganshire Canal, which ran under Kingsway. It was hit by a German incendiary bomb in March 1941 and was destroyed. (The Royal Photographic Company, London)

2

Central Cardiff

Cardiff has always been a city of change and as early as the 1860s residents of the town were complaining about the many changes that were taking place. The postcard pictures in this section provide us with more than a glimpse of the long-gone places and faces. One exception is the New Theatre, built in 1906 and still providing a varied and rich assortment of entertainment.

The famous Cardiff Arms Park can be seen to the left of this aerial view of the Civic Centre, taken before the Westgate Street flats had been built in around 1930. (Aerofilms Ltd)

The Cardiff Free Library, now the home of the Cardiff Museum, was opened by Mayor Alford Thomas on 31 May 1896. St John's Church is seen on the left of the picture, in around 1904. (Raphael Tuck & Sons)

The much loved David Morgan family store on The Hayes closed its doors in January 2005, having provided thousands of customers with unrivalled service for 125 years. This card is from around 1905. (The Strand Series)

Westgate Street, looking towards Wood Street. The Jackson Hall is to the right of picture. This card is from around 1880. (Ernest T. Bush)

A view of Duke Street in 1922. The Street was widened in 1924 and a row of shops, abutting on the castle wall, were knocked down. The earliest form of the name suggests the association with ducks or poulterers' shops. (The Royal Photographic Company, London)

The year is 1887 and the people in this picture are standing outside the Savings Bank in North Street, which was renamed Kingsway in 1909. (Ernest T. Bush)

The East Canal Wharf from St Mary Street. The Central Hotel on the extreme right of the picture was destroyed in a fire in 2003. This card is from around 1910. (Ernest T. Bush)

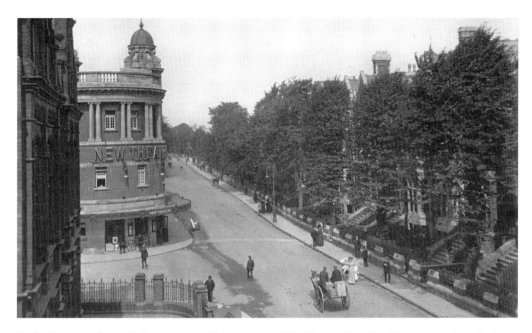

Park Place was formally known as Dobbinpitts and Blind Lane. The New Theatre on the left of the picture was built in 1906 by London architects Messrs Runtz and Ford. (The Royal Photographic Company, London)

Fitzhamon Embankment. Cardiff Bridge, popularly known as Canton Bridge, can be seen in the distance. Robert Fitzhamon (1093–1107) was one of the Lords of Cardiff. This card is from around 1911. (The Royal Photographic Company, London)

The University College was situated in the town end of Newport Road, and was at one time an infirmary. This card is from around 1900. (Dainty Series)

Queen Street Railway Station in Station Terrace. It was originally a wooden structure dating from 1840. It was rebuilt in 1887, before a stone building was built in 1954. (C.B. Swallow)

The Central Post Office in Westgate Street stood on the site of Hutchinsons & Tayleur's Wooden Circus Theatre. It was situated opposite the *Western Mail* & *South Wales Echo* offices. (The Wrench Series)

Electric trams came to Cardiff on 2 May 1902, and by 1905 there were 131 trams carrying the citizens of Cardiff to their places of work and pleasure. This one is seen in Queen Street. (Pamlin Prints)

The Glamorganshire Canal was opened in 1794 as a means of transporting iron from Merthyr to Cardiff Docks. Twenty-five miles long, it had fifty-two locks; this one is at North Road. This card is from around 1910. (Ernest T. Bush)

3

Civic Centre

The central area of Cardiff has experienced a complete rejuvenation with landmarks such as the Millennium Stadium, the new Central Library and the St David's shopping centre all springing up over the past ten years or so. Luxury apartments have replaced the little terraced houses, demolished in the 1950s, and the half-a-dozen or so cinemas that used to be in Queen Street. However, the magnificent civic centre, with its famous buildings and statues, is a constant reminder of the city's historic past.

From *Cardiff Notes: Picturesque And Biographical* by J. Kyrle Fletcher:

In Cathays Park is a group of civic buildings well known to those who study civic development in its rougher aspects, a group which alone would completely justify a visit of inspection to this city. In many of our towns fine examples of modern architecture may be found, but it is indeed rare in these islands to find a group of buildings serving various civic, county and national needs grouped together with such considerable harmony on one site.

(Aerofilms Series)

The magnificent equestrian statue of the 1st Viscount Lord Tredegar mounted on his charger, Sir Briggs, was designed by the world-famous sculptor Sir William Goscombe John. It was unveiled in 1909, in the presence of Lord Tredegar, on the fifty-fifth anniversary of the day he lead a troup of Lancers in the Charge of the Light Brigade at Balaclava. This card is from around 1920. (The Strand Series)

The splendid City Hall, designed by Messrs Lanchester and Rickards, was erected in 1906. The two groups of statuary flanking the window in the centre depict the sea receiving the three rivers of Cardiff – The Taff, Rhymney and Ely. (The Grosvenor Series, posted 1915)

The Law Courts, on the left of the picture, was also designed by Lanchester, Steward and Rickards and the eastern façade is surmounted by two beautifully designed cupolas. (Ernest T. Bush)

The 194ft high clock tower and dome with the Welsh dragon on top is a feature of this beautiful Portland stone building. (Real Photograph)

The present-day City Hall is the fifth to serve as Cardiff's centre of local government. (Valentine's & Sons Ltd, posted 1964)

The Law Courts were skilfully designed so as to be in harmony with the City Hall. When this picture was taken, the statue of Judge Gwilym Williams of Miskin, which now stands in front of the building, had yet to be erected. (Raphael Tuck & Sons)

The man and woman in this picture postcard are passing the statue of Judge Gwilym Williams (1839-1906), Stipendiary Judge and Squire. It was sculpted by Cardiff's William Goscombe John. (Real Photograph, posted 1960)

Designed by W.D. Carew, 'the new' University Building College was opened in 1909, when only the main front and library were ready for the official opening. (The City Series)

Built on a five-acre site on the east side of Cathays Park, University College had been established in Newport Road in 1883. The statue of its first president, Henry Austin Bruce, stands in Alexandra Gardens, facing the present administrative headquarters of the college. (Ernest T. Bush)

The large sculptured groups in front of the main façade of the Glamorgan County Hall were designed by Albert Hodge and represent mining and navigation. The architects were Harris and Moodi and the building was opened in 1912. (Real Photograph, posted 1954)

To the left of the picture is the Cardiff Technical College, later known as the University Registry. Designed in the style of the English Renaissance, it was enlarged in 1931 by the architect T. Alwyn Lloyd. It was built around an open courtyard. (Photochrom Co. Ltd)

Unveiled by General Sir John French on 29 November 1909, the South African war memorial is dedicated to the Welshmen who fell in South Africa 1899-1902. It bears the names of nearly 200 Welsh soldiers who died in the conflict. (*Western Mail & Echo Ltd*)

The National War Memorial of Wales, in Alexandra Gardens, was unveiled by Edward, Prince of Wales on 12 June 1928. Its main features are three bronze statues of a sailor, a soldier and an airman. (British Manufacture)

Designed by H.N. Comper, the Welsh National War Memorial was going to be situated on the circular green in front of the City Hall, but both the City Council and Museum authorities objected to the proposed site. (Postcard publisher unidentified)

NATIONAL MUSEUM OF WALES & TREDEGAR STATUE, CARDIFF.

The foundation stone of the National Museum of Wales was laid by His Majesty King George V on 26 June 1912. But the main block and western galleries were not opened until 1927, owing to the First World War. (Postcard publisher unidentified)

The eastern wing and the Reardon-Smith Lecture Theatre were not finished until 1932. (Postcard publisher unidentified, posted 1927)

From *Great Welshmen of Modern Days* by Sir Thomas Hughes:

Judge Gwilym Williams – The crowning glory of the man was his ardent love for his nation, its tradition, its people, its music, its poetry, its language, its life, which he touches with every facet.

(Raphael Tuck & Sons)

The life-sized bronze statue in Gorsedd Gardens is that of Lord Ninian Crichton-Stuart, MP for Cardiff. He was killed in action at the Battle of Loos during the First World War. (M.J.R.B)

The statue of philanthropist and coal owner John Cory in front of the City Hall, like the statues of Lord Tredegar and Lord Ninian Stuart, it is the work of Sir William Goscombe John. (Ernest T. Bush)

4

School Days

A few of the picture postcards in this chapter date from living memory and some Cardiffians will recognise their parents – or even grandparents – as school children in the smiling young faces of these pupils of the past.

Children from Frederick Street and Canal Street line up in Williams Court to have their pictures taken before setting off on a day trip to Porthcawl. The picture was taken just after the Second World War. The lady on the extreme left is Mrs Sarah Donovan, who lived at No. 59 Frederick Street. (Supersnaps)

The famous Cardiff Snowflakes Choir winners, at Llangollen in 1947 and 1949, of the International singing contest. (Postcard publisher unidentified)

Empire Day celebrations at Roath Park School in 1909. Note the piano on left of the picture. (A & G Taylor's Pictorial Postcard, Duke Street Arcade, Cardiff)

Roath Park Primary School. The teacher on the left of the picture is believed to be Miss Lancaster. This card is from around 1925. (Postcard publisher unidentified)

Moorland Road School. The teacher on the right of the picture is believed to be Mr Moses. This card is from around 1920. (Postcard publisher unidentified)

Another 1920s postcard picture of Moorland Road School pupils. Teacher Mr Joshua can be seen on the right of the picture. (Postcard publisher unidentified)

This Gladstone School postcard picture, taken during the First World War, shows pupils attending a woodwork class. (Postcard publisher unidentified)

'Thank Heaven for Little Girls!' Stacey Road School, Class 2. The picture is thought to have been taken around 1923. (Postcard publisher unidentified)

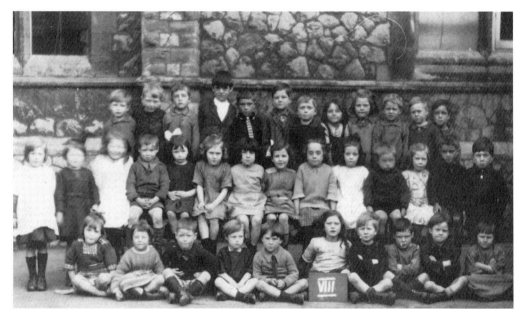

Another unidentified postcard picture showing the boys and girls who attended Adamsdown School in the early 1920s. (Postcard publisher unidentified)

Crwys Road Board School. The school was closed in 1939 and during the war American soldiers were billeted there. It later became the College of Food Technology and is now a supermarket. This picture was taken in 1917. (Postcard publisher unidentified)

Roath Park Elementary School. The picture was apparently taken in 1929, and some ten or twelve years later some of these pupils would have found themselves in the Armed Forces. (British Made)

Patricia Evans, aged thirteen, of Maria Street in Welsh National Costume. Later known as Mrs Pat Collins, she died, aged eighty-six, in 2010. A true Cardiffian, she was a great friend of co-author Brian Lee. (Postcard publisher unidentified)

The Cardiff Schoolboys Football Team of 1927. Eight members of the team came from either Kitchener Road School or Moorland Road School. (Postcard publisher unidentified)

The pupils from St Cuthbert's and St Patrick's Schools who attended the Silver Jubilee Camp, Porthcawl, in 1950. Seated in the centre is the warden, Mr Gwylym Lewis. (Gordon R. Thomas)

The Roath Park School soccer team in 1925-1926. The teacher on the left of the picture is wearing a bow tie, which apparently was the fashion in those days. (Postcard publisher unidentified)

St Peter's Roman Catholic School, Class 1. The boy on the top row, second from the left, is author Brian Lee. The school has now been demolished and a block of flats is now situated on the site. This card is from around 1942. (Postcard publisher unidentified)

A fancy dress competition was held for the children in Dalton Street as part of the 1953 Coronation Day celebrations. The girl standing to the left of the gentleman is Jacqueline Bryant, who lived at No. 37 Dalton Street. (Postcard publisher unidentified)

There were enough Grange Council School pupils in this picture to make more than four soccer teams! Three of the boys are holding footballs. This card is from around 1930. (Postcard publisher unidentified)

Pupils of St Iltyd's College – though only two or three of them seem to be wearing their school blazers! This card is from around 1944. (Postcard publisher unidentified)

Marlborough Road Primary School pupils in around 1930. (Postcard publisher unidentified)

Grangetown School pupils of 1932. The teacher wearing plus fours is Mr Ivor Beynon. (Postcard publisher unidentified)

St Mary's School, Clarence Road, Docks. The boys appear to outnumber the girls. Alan Ingram can be seen in the third row down and fifth from the right. This card is from around 1932. (Postcard publisher unidentified)

5

St Mary Street

From *Cardiff Notes: Picturesque And Biographical* by J. Kyrle Fletcher:

From the Bute Monument, by the Great Western Railway Station, to the castle, nearly half a mile away, runs a broad straight street, the widest and, historically, the most interesting street in the City of Cardiff. It is named St Mary's Street, after a famous old church which once stood at the monument end, but in the year of the Great Flood, 1607, the river which ran just behind the street – whereas it now runs in its new bed two hundred yards away – bursting over with its flood waters, tore down the principal Church of the borough of Cardiff.

The Panopticon Playhouse Theatre used to be situated on the left of picture and on the extreme right once stood four pubs right next door to each other; these were the Royal Oak, The Blue Anchor, Elliots Hotel and The Terminus. (Real Photograph, posted 1923)

The Great Western Hotel, on the left of the picture, was built in French Gothic style in 1876 and had several changes of name over the years. (Grosvenor Series, posted 1913)

The Terminus Hotel, on the right, was originally called the Steam Mill Arms. It later became The Terminus and was known as Sam's Bar in the 1990s. It was renamed Zync in 2005. (Valentine & Sons Ltd)

The Sandringham Hotel, on the left of the picture, was established in 1792, when it was known as The Black Lion. It became The Sandringham in 1902. On the opposite side of the picture the South Wales News offices can be seen. (The R.A Postcards Ltd, London)

The shop on the left of the picture, which is on the corner of Church Street and St Mary Street, was once the residence of Squire John Richards, a well-known landowner. When this picture was taken it was Edwin Dobson's Stationery shop. (Raphael Tuck & Sons, posted 25 March 1905)

On the right of the picture is James Howell & Co's Family Store, now part of the House of Fraser group. On the extreme left is the Queens Hotel, which closed in 1974. (Valentine & Sons Ltd)

The old Town Hall, opened in 1853, was situated on the west side of St Mary Street. It replaced the Guild Hall, which was in the middle of High Street. It included a Post Office and a police court. (Alfred Freke, Cardiff, posted July 1906)

The Royal Hotel, on the left, was opened in 1866 and extended in 1890. The Theatre Royal public house opposite was established in 1883. (E.T. Bush)

Almost directly above the man looking towards the camera is a sign for D'Arc's Waxworks Exhibition, later known as the Cardiff Continental Waxworks. It closed in 1946 and many of the exhibits ended up at Coney Beach fairground, Porthcawl. (Raphael Tuck & Sons)

The new Theatre Royal stood on the corner of St Mary Street and Wood Street. It was gutted by a fire in 1899 and was known as the Playhouse in 1920 and the Prince of Wales in 1935. (The Camera Series, *Western Mail*, Cardiff)

The statue of John, 2nd Marquis of Bute, was erected in High Street, facing the castle, in 1853 and was moved to the southern end of St Mary Street in 1879. It was later relocated to Callaghan Square. (Raphael Tuck & Sons)

From The *Evening Press*:

On 1 May 1902, Cardiff Corporation Electric Tramways were successfully opened for traffic, amidst the general rejoicing of everyone concerned.

(Photochrom Co. Ltd, posted October 1927)

On the extreme left of picture is the third home of the *Western Mail & Evening Express* office. Opened in 1895, papers were produced there until 1930. (H. Tempest, Ltd)

The entrance to the Central Market can be seen, right of the picture, between the two horse and carriages. The original façade, which houses the underpass into the market, was built in 1884 and was known as 'Solomon's Temple' after ' Solly Andrews'. (E.T. Bush)

From *Cardiff Notes: Picturesque And Biographical* by J. Kyrle Fletcher:

Once upon a time St Mary Street was made up of the town houses of the local gentry. Lewis of the Van, Mathews of Llandaff, Basset of Beau Pr'e. Both had their office and town residence to which they would come during the winter months.

(Postcard publisher unidentified)

6

Queen Street

From *Cardiff Notes: Picturesque And Biographical* by J. Kyrle Fletcher:

Queen Street is a modern name given to an old street in honour of Queen Victoria, but I like its old name better: Crockherbtown. This was the vegetable market, the haunt of many market gardeners who lived there and had big market gardens behind their houses.

By resolution of the town council, Crockherbtown became Queen Street in December 1886. The long gone Tivoli Hotel can be on the seen on the right of the picture. This card is from around 1906. (Valentine & Sons Ltd)

The Principality Building Society with its clock tower was built on the site of St John's Schools. Built in 1913, it has recently been refurbished. (The Photochrom Co. Ltd, posted 1915)

Back in 1853, an unsuccessful attempt was made to change the name of Queen Street to Park Street. In 1862, a number of old buildings were demolished and the street was widened. (The Photochrom Co. Ltd, posted 1924)

The Empire Theatre, with its large dome and circular glass window, was described as 'an architectural triumph'. Opened in 1887 as Levino's Hall, it later became a cinema and was demolished in 1962, to make way for C&A Stores. (Raphael Tuck & Sons, posted 1910)

Said to resemble a watered-down version of the Louvre in Paris, the Park Hotel opened in 1885 and is now known as The Parc. Queen Street was pedestrianised in 1958. (Valentine's & Sons Ltd, posted 1918)

R.E. Jones' The Carlton Restaurant, in the centre of the picture, was a popular venue for wining, dining, and dancing in the 1920s and 1930s. It was bombed during the last war and British Homestores later occupied the site. (Temple Series)

Trolley buses – note the wires – first came into service in Cardiff in 1942 and the last one ran from Wood Street to Llandaff Fields in 1966. The store with the pillars, on the left is Marments Ltd, which closed in 1986. (Raphael Tuck & Sons Ltd)

7

Parks and Open Spaces

There cannot be many towns or cities in the United Kingdom that possess as many parks and open spaces as Cardiff. There are more than 2,700 acres of parks in the Welsh capital. The city's Roath Park, opened in 1894, has 98 acres, while Heath Park has 84 acres; Heol Trelai, the former Ely Racecourse has 86 acres, Cefn On has an impressive 205 acres, while Bute Park, which is also known as the Castle Grounds in Coopers Fields, has a massive 350 acres.

Roath Park was opened to the public on 20 June 1894. The Great Western Railway ran cheap excursions from Swansea, Cheltenham and Bristol for the opening. Cardiff was brought almost to a standstill. Shops closed and thousands lined the route of the carriage procession. (Temple, Real Photo Series)

It took seven years to transform the malarial bog known as the Kenelechi into the beautiful park it is today. Before the construction of Roath Park, much of the area was used as common land by gypsies. This card is from around 1920. (Valentine & Sons Ltd)

Hundreds of people used to flock to the bandstand to listen to the music every Sunday. In the 1930s, open-air dancing was staged in the park and between 5,000-6,000 people enjoyed the music. (The Royal Photographic Company, posted 1911)

The Captain Robert Falcon Scott memorial lighthouse tower was erected in 1915. Scott reached the Antarctic on the 18 January 1912, but died on the return journey just a few miles from basecamp. (The Grosvenor Series, posted September 1917)

In Edwardian times as many as 2,000 bathers could be seen swimming in the lake on Sunday mornings. But no mixed bathing was allowed, and the ladies and gentlemen had their own bathing sections. The Roath Park annual aquatic carnival included rowing, as well as swimming events and 'crazy races' such as the plank and shovel race. (Valentine & Sons Ltd)

The annual Taff Swim moved to Roath Park Lake in 1931, until pollution of the lake rendered swimming off-limits thirty years later. In 1912 a number of boys were summoned before the Cardiff stipendiary for bathing in Roath Park Lake without proper attire and received cautions and fines ranging up to 2s 6d. (Ernest T. Bush)

The Islands of Roath Park are out of bounds to boats these days. Lord Tredegar presented eight pairs of 'dinky ducks' which were placed to rest on the islands. (The Grosvenor Series)

The bathing huts can be seen behind the Captain Scott memorial lighthouse in this view of the promenade from the 1950s. (Valentine & Sons Ltd, posted 20 August 1954)

On 8 April 1895, Councillor G. Beynon Harris brought forward a motion in favour of permitting boating on Roath Park Lake on Sundays. But a Nonconformist deputation protested against the proposal, and the motion was defeated. Wooden boats on the lake were once maintained with wood from trees taken from Cefn Onn Park. (Valentine & Sons Ltd)

During the Second World War, railings around the lake were melted down for munitions. Roath Park is one of Wales' most popular tourist destinations and attracts around 2 million visitors a year. This card is from around 1910. (E.T. Bush; The Royal Photographic Company)

Shortly after Roath Park was opened to the public, notices were placed around the park offering a reward of £5 for 'such information as will lead to a conviction of any persons shooting wildfowl.' (Postcard publisher unidentified, posted 15 May 1924)

As well as concerts, Roath Park has staged all kind of events over the years from plays and carnivals to open-air dances which attracted as many as 6,000 people. This card is from around 1920. (The Grosvenor Series)

More than fifty species of waterfowl are resident on the lake and wild islands. Weymouth Corporation presented six of their royal swans to Roath Park Lake a year after it opened in 1895. This card is from around 1925. (Valentine's & Sons Ltd)

Roath Park in full bloom. The Conservatory in Roath Park houses hundreds of exotic plants, while the rose beds are ablaze with colour each summer. (Ozograph Series, Bristol)

Whitchurch Common. During the Second World War, the 2nd Evacuation Unit of the United States Army set up a tented camp on the land. This card is from around 1950. (H. Tempest, Ltd)

A plaque commemorating the planting of trees seen in this picture reads: 'This Avenue of trees was planted on behalf of the 2nd Evacuation Unit of the United States Army as a token of gratitude for the hospitality extended to them by the parishioners of Whitchurch during the Second World War, 1939-1945'. This card is from around 1950. (Valentine & Sons Ltd)

Some of the most sought-after houses in Cardiff are those in Plasturton Gardens. These were built in the 1890s. (The Royal Photographic Company)

Sophia Gardens was opened to the public in 1857, and the *Cardiff and Merthyr Guardian* described it as 'an ornamental walk and pleasure ground of exquisite taste in design, which for its extent and magnificence will be unparalleled by anything of the sort in Wales'. (The Grosvenor Series)

From *Cardiff Notes: Picturesque And Biographical* by J. Kyrle Fletcher:

Gorsedd Gardens, Cathays Park – In front of the National Museum building is a flower garden, and on the green turf is a circle of rough unhewn stones, the Gorsedd Circle of the Bards of the Island of Britain.

(British Manufacture, posted August 1938)

Queen Alexandra Gardens, Cathays Park. The statue on the left depicts Henry Austin Bruce, the 1st Lord of Aberdare and the first president of the University of Wales. The statue was originally unveiled in Howard Gardens in 1899 and moved to its present location in 1914. This card is from around 1920. (Valentine & Sons Ltd)

This statue in Friary Gardens is of the 3rd Marquis of Bute. It was designed by Dr P. MacGillivray and unveiled in 1930. Almost certainly the richest man in the world at that time, he died in 1900. This card is from around 1950. (Raphael Tuck & Sons Ltd)

Victoria Park was 'thrown open to the public on Wednesday, 16 June 1897'. In 1919 the parks committee accepted a gift of a tank, and on another occasion two captured German field artillery guns were also on display there. (*Western Mail* Ltd, Cardiff, posted 1904)

The first park in Cardiff to have a bandstand was Grange Gardens. It was erected in 1895 and was demolished some years ago. This popular little park now has a new bandstand. The war memorial can be seen to the right of the picture. This card is from around 1920. (Postcard publisher unidentified)

In 1911 Charles Thompson gave Canton's Thompson Park to Cardiff. The 'boy with a butterfly' statue is called Joyance and it has been sadly stolen and damaged on a number of occasions. This card is from around 1930. (Stewart & Woolf, London, E.C.)

The Wenallt Rhiwbina. A wonderful view of Cardiff and the Bristol Channel before the reservoir in the foreground was covered over. This card is from around 1950. (Griffiths & Sutton Ltd)

The Rhiwbina Village Green. Before the First World War there were few houses in Rhiwbina, the area being populated by a number of large farms. It wasn't until 1974 that Rhiwbina became a suburb of Cardiff. This card is from around 1935. (T.H. Spear, Rhiwbina, near Cardiff)

8

Sporting Moments

No book devoted to picture postcards of Cardiff would be complete without a section or chapter on the part sport has played in the city and life of its citizens. Be it in the boxing ring, on the football pitch or in the swimming pool, Cardiff has produced a number of sporting greats. Some, including Peerless Jim Driscoll, Paulo Radmilovic, David Broome, and Fred Keenor, are depicted in the following pages.

This rare picture postcard shows the start of the second annual Docks Temperance Institute Marathon Race, which took place on Good Friday, 25 March 1910. (Metropole Studios, Cardiff)

Cardiff's Barney Johnson held a number of walking-race records in the 1930s. (British Made)

St Saviour's Harrier's cross-country
team, 1912. (Postcard publisher
unidentified)

T. Harry, of St Saviour's, who
represented Wales at cross-country
running in 1910. He was also
a winner of the Welsh Junior
Cross-Country Championship. This
card is from around 1912. (Postcard
publisher unidentified)

Another notable cross-country runner was J. Parker, of Cathays Harriers. (Postcard publisher unidentified)

The Cardiff Dragons speedway team. During the 1950s, speedway took place at the Penarth Road Stadium. Thousands of fans would flock to the stadium on Thursday nights to cheer home their favourite riders. This card is from around 1952. (H. Tempest, Ltd)

The Cardiff University boxing team, 1930. Unfortunately their names are not known. (Postcard publisher unidentified)

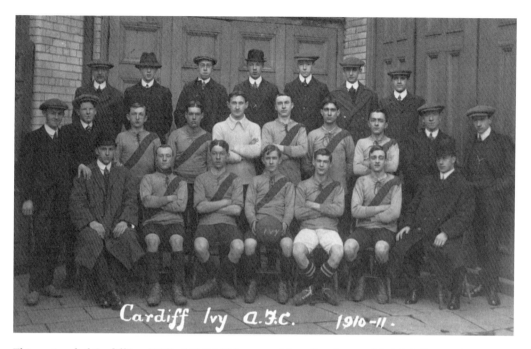

This postcard of Cardiff Ivy AFC in 1910-1911 was sent from London to a Mr D.J. Williams of Moorland Road, Cardiff, but the team remains something of a mystery. (A & G Taylor, posted 7 March 1911)

Cardiff City, 1st Team, 1920-1921. Fred Keenor (1894-1972), who captained the team to victory over Arsenal in the 1927 FA Cup, is pictured on the extreme right of the back row. (Postcard publisher unidentified)

The Cardiff City team which won the 1927 FA Cup. The team was dubbed The Bluebirds – but no one really knows why! (Postcard publisher unidentified)

Cardiff City Ladies AFC, 1918-1919. There are no records of Cardiff City having a ladies' team, so this surely was a joke postcard! (Postcard publisher unidentified)

Adamsdown School soccer team in 1920. The gentleman wearing a trilby looks very much like Lord
Glanely! (Gale's Studios Ltd)

The Moorland Road School team, who defeated Radnor Road School in the Seager Cup, 1932-1933.
Seated third from the left is Harry Pressdee. The match took place at the Welsh White City stadium at
Sloper Road. (McGlenn, No.2A Plantagnet St, Cardiff)

Cardiff swimmer Paulo Radmilovic (1886-1968), who won gold medals at the Olympic Games of 1908, 1912 and 1920. This card is from around 1908. (Health & Strength Series)

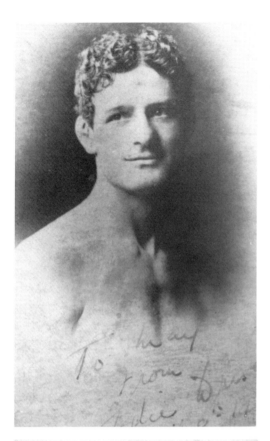

Cardiff boxer Peerless Jim Driscoll (1880-1925). One hundred thousand people lined the streets of Cardiff when his funeral procession wound its way to Cathays Cemetery. (Postcard publisher unidentified)

Welsh champion swimmer W.J. Kimber held a number of swimming records but lived in the shadow of Paulo Radmilovic. This card is from around 1925. (T.L.C.)

The text on the left side of the picture
reads: W. Kimber. CAPT. WALES.
100YDS & ½ MILE CHAMPION.
1912. This card is from around 1925.
(T.L.C.)

World and European show-jumping
champion David Broome – seen here
on Wildfire III – was born in the
Fairwater district of Cardiff. (Valentine
& Sons Ltd)

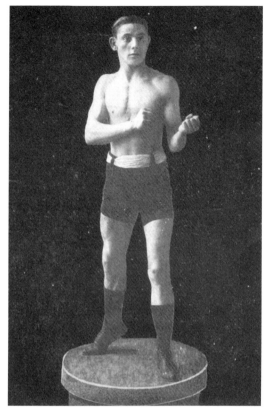

Above left: Cardiff boxer Boyo Driscoll (1884-1966) – no relation to Jim Driscoll. He defeated future world bantam king Owen Moran at Cardiff in 1904. (*Western Mail* Ltd, Cardiff)

Above: Cardiff boxer Joe Erskine (1934-1990) was British Heavyweight Champion from 1956-1958 and Empire Heavyweight Champion from 1957-1958. (Craely, Cardiff)

'King of the Road'. Walker Dai Barry won numerous Welsh championship titles in the 1950s. His son Steve won a gold medal at the 1982 Commonwealth Games in Brisbane, smashing the old Commonwealth Games record by nearly twelve minutes. (Postcard publisher unidentified)

9

Suburbs

From *Cardiff Notes: Picturesque And Biographical* by J. Kyrle Fletcher:

Visits to some of these places have been to me very happy pilgrimages. To some I have walked, which after all is the ideal way to go out and search the picturesque. Give me a good companion, a pair of comfortable boots, and I care not if it rains or snows.

The church on the left of the picture is the Roath Road Wesleyan Methodist Church, which was opened in 1871 and was almost demolished when bombed during the Second World War. St James' Church, on the right, was consecrated on 15 June 1894 and was closed quite recently. This card is from around 1905. (Raphael Tuck & Sons)

Newport Road, an ancient highway, was once known as Roath Road and the villas built there in the 1850s have now been replaced with offices and a hotel. This card is from around 1905. (Philco Series)

The houses in Ninian Road, Roath, date from 1891. The road was named after the second son of the 3rd Marquis of Bute. Roath Park recreation fields are situated on the right of the picture and the iron railings have long since gone. (Ernest T. Bush, posted 1915)

The staff of Rees & Gwillam's corner shop posed for this picture in 1905. The shop was situated on the corner of Penylan Road and Blenheim Road. (Croydon Collectorcard)

The area of land near the junction between Crwys Road, City Road and Albany Road was in ancient times known as The Gallows Field. A plaque on the side of the wall of the National Westminster Bank reads, 'On this site on the 22 July, 1679, Father Phillip Evans and Father John Lloyd were executed for exercising their priestly duties. Declared Saints and Martyrs by Pope Paul VI on 25 October, 1970.' (*Western Mail* Ltd, posted 1904)

This was how Clifton Street looked in 1909. It used to be known as Connection Street but its name was changed on 5 May, 1868. (Postcard publisher unidentified)

'Give my regards to Broadway'. This Broadway has no connection with the one in the song. It used to be known as Green Lane. This card is from around 1910. (Postcard publisher unidentified)

Romilly Crescent Canton. In the distance can be seen the steeple of Conway Road Methodist Church. The picture was taken in 1906 and the horse-drawn trams are those of Solly Andrews. (E. J. Colley, Romilly Crescent Post Office)

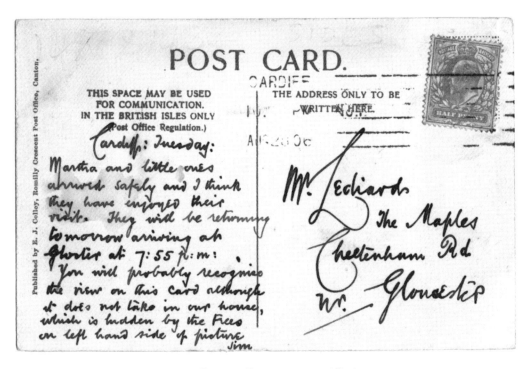

Reverse side of the card above. (E. J. Colley, Romilly Crescent Post Office)

The spire of St John the Evangelist Church can be seen in the distance of this postcard scene, of the Municipal Secondary School in Canton, later known as Canton High School. This card is from around 1910. (Ernest T. Bush)

The neo-Jacobean Plymouth Arms, on the left of the picture, is well situated for visitors to the Museum of Welsh Life and St Fagans Castle. (Postcard publisher unidentified)

From *The Illustrated History of Cardiff Suburbs* by Dennis Morgan:

The first important public building in Riverside was the Union Workhouse in Cowbridge Road. Opened in 1836, it was a place where only the desperate sought refuge. To obtain parish relief, the whole family had to enter the workhouse. Men were sent to one ward, wives and children to another, and their meetings were restricted to 45 minutes a day. The regime was monotonous and hard. Men chopped wood, broke stones or carried coal, while the women worked in the laundry, helped to clean the building, or picked oakum. By 1900 the regime was less harsh. Many families were able to avoid the workhouse regime, as the authorities granted them a few shillings a week in outdoor relief, the forerunner of the retirement pension and unemployment benefit. Within the workhouse, trusted inmates were allowed out so long as they returned by 7pm, thereby avoiding the temptation of alcohol. In time the workhouse became a hospital, changing its name first to the City Lodge and then St David's Hospital. The site has now been redeveloped to provide a smaller hospital and housing accommodation, though the façade of the old building remains.

(Ernest T. Bush)

Cardiff Road, Llandaff. This pretty postcard scene was taken in August 1894. A milk churn can be seen in the horse-cart. (Ernest T. Bush)

Beulah Road, Rhiwbina. The first shop on the left was an ironmonger's run by Mr & Mrs Gooch. It later became a dry cleaner's shop. (Valentine & Sons Ltd, posted 18 August 1958)

The houses in Merthyr Road, Whitchurch, on the left of picture, have made way for shops. (Ernest T. Bush)

The sign on the house reads: S.M. Henson & Son Ladies Hairdressers. This card is from around 1950. (Valentine & Sons Ltd)

The brook in Tyn-Y-Parc Road, on the left of the picture, is known as Nant Waedlyd. It has been suggested that the young man in the picture is Ernest T. Bush himself! (Ernest T. Bush)

Park Road, Whitchurch. Note the telegraph poles. (Ernest T. Bush)

Whitchurch Free Library, built in 1904, was designed by Messrs R. & S. Williams and built by Mr W.T. Morgan, at a cost of £2,000. (Ernest T. Bush)

The children of Milwards Terrace posed for this picture in Merthyr Road. (Ernest T. Bush)

Heol Don Road, Whitchurch. Not much traffic about when this picture was taken! (Postcard publisher unidentified)

Whitchurch Railway Station. The station was used during the First World War to bring wounded servicemen, by ambulance-train, to Whitchurch Military Hospital. (Postcard publisher unidentified)

Dan Murphy outside his newsagent's shop in Adam Street. The *News Chronicle* poster reads 'Britain's Black-Out Plans – OFFICIAL', while at the Capitol Cinema, George O'Brien was starring in the 1939 film *The Painted Desert*. (Postcard publisher unidentified)

Llanishen Village. St Isan's Parish Church can be seen in the distance. (Valentine & Sons Ltd)

City Road, originally known as Heol-Y-Plwcca, was later called Castle Road. It became City Road when Cardiff became a city in 1905. (Croydon Collectorcard)

Woodville Road, in Cathays, was named after Colonel Wood, who built several streets in the area, the chief one being Woodville Road. The Coronet Cinema, which closed in 1972, was situated on the extreme right, on the corner. This card is from around 1904. (Collector Card)

Park Road, Whitchurch. The shops may be different, but Park Road has changed little since this picture was taken in the 1950s. (Valentine & Sons Ltd)

The houses on the left of picture are in Milward's Terrace (87-111 Merthyr Road), This card is from around 1950. (Valentine & Sons Ltd)

The bridge across the River Taff is often referred to as Canton Bridge, but its real name is Cardiff Bridge. It dates from around 1790 but was rebuilt and opened in 1931 by the Marchioness of Bute. (M.J.R – B)

This postcard of Cardiff Bridge is from an original water colour by B.F.C. Parr. The original medieval timbered bridge was replaced by a stone bridge. (Valentine & Sons Ltd)

Looking towards Coryton, this postcard picture shows Heath Halt (low station). Both sides of the railway are now dotted with houses. This card is from around 1920. (Ernest T. Bush)

The first batch of houses in the Rhiwbina Village Company was completed in June 1914. (T.H.Spear, Rhiwbina, near Cardiff)

The churchyard at Llandaff Cathedral. The north churchyard was first used for burial in 1883. This card is from around 1920. (Postcard publisher unidentified)

10

The Docklands

When Cardiff Docks was being built in the 1830s, many migrant workers were attracted to the area. By the late 1890s, Cardiff was Britain's largest coal-exporting port. But the decline of the coal and iron industries in the 1960s and 1970s sounded the death-knell for the docklands and by the 1980s the area had become a scene of dereliction. But, just like the phoenix that rose from the ashes, Cardiff Docks has become Cardiff Bay, where the National Assembly's parliament house, the Senedd and other fine buildings now stand.

The Bute West Dock, on the right of the picture, was opened on 9 October 1839. A single-track railway line crossed over the Inner Lock by a swing bridge. This card is from around 1900. (Ernest T. Bush)

Sailing ships were still in vogue when the Roath Basin Dock was built in 1869. The entrance lock was 350ft long and 80ft wide. This card is from around 1900. (Viner & Co.)

The Queen Alexandra Dock was opened on 13 July 1907, by King Edward VII and Queen Alexandra. The entrance lock was 850ft long and 90ft wide. (Postcard publisher unidentified)

The Low Water Pier – which has long since disappeared. The sign left of pier reads: MAXIMUM SPEED EIGHT MILES AN HOUR. This card is from around 1900. (Postcard publisher unidentified)

The imposing Pierhead Building, which opened as the new dock offices on August Bank Holiday Monday, 1897. Designed by William Frame, this grade II listed building, with its terracotta tile work, is perhaps Cardiff Bay's most famous landmark. (Raphael Tuck & Sons, posted 13 September 1910)

P&A Campbell pleasure steamers sailed from the Pierhead Building between 1886 and 1972. They later sailed from Penarth Pier. This card is from around 1900. (Ernest T. Bush)

The Sailors' Home was situated in Stuart Street and was financed by the Marquis of Bute. It was opened shortly after it was built in 1856. (Osbourne Long)

Clarence Road Bridge was opened by the Duke of Clarence in September 1890. The meccano-like structure was demolished in the 1970s and replaced with a more modern bridge in 1976. This card is from around 1905. (Croydon Collectors)

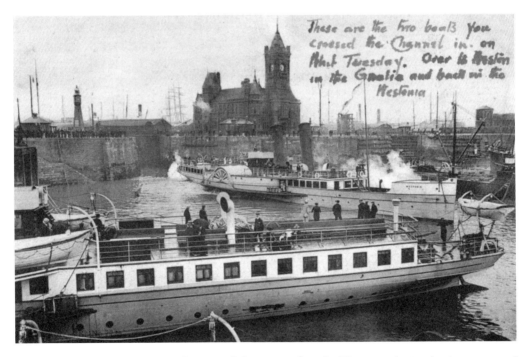

The message in the top right-hand corner of this postcard reads: 'These are the two boats you crossed the channel in, on that Tuesday. Over to Weston in the *Gwalia* and back in the *Westonia*'. This card is from around 1905. (Postcard publisher unidentified)

'The days of the old windjammers – otherwise known as sailing ships – seem to have left us for ever. Often as a boy I have stood on Cardiff Pier Head and witnessed the sailing of long ships,' wrote a correspondent to a local paper in 1927. (J.B. & E. Rolls, Warwick Library, Cardiff, posted 23 February 1908)

It was in 1964 that the Bute West Dock finished trading and six years later, in 1970, it was filled in. Ships, like this one in the 1880s, would have been under the control of William Thomas Lewis, the general manager. (G.D. & D.L., posted 1906)

11

Memorable Moments

Royal visits, Corpus Christi processions, and 'after the war' street parties are some of the special and memorable occasions that are recalled in this chapter.

The occasion was the opening of the Queen Alexandra Dock in 1907. This parade of Cardiff school children gathers under Bute Street Bridge. (Postcard publisher unidentified)

The Lord Mayor of Cardiff, Alderman William Crossman, is knighted by King Edward VII, on 13 July 1907. (A.W. Sargent, Albany Road, Cardiff)

The streets were lined with flags and bunting for the occasion. The Great Western Railway Station is to the left of the picture. (The Mezzotint Co., Brighton)

The crowd cheer and wave as the royal party pass Billy Kitchin's ship chandlers in Bute Street. (Postcard publisher unidentified)

The Cardiff Photographic Society annual outing. This card is from around 1935. (Postcard publisher unidentified)

Workers' Union Cardiff, No.7 Branch Committee and Officials, 5 November 1921. The only lady in the picture can be seen seated in the centre of the front row. (Postcard publisher unidentified)

Residents of Bertram Street, in Broadway, pose for the photographer on the occasion of the Coronation of King George VI, in 1937. (Postcard publisher unidentified)

The residents of Hewell Street, in Grangetown, who took part in a fancy dress competition as part of the 1937 Coronation celebrations. (Postcard publisher unidentified)

Rag week in the 1920s. These students, from the Cardiff Technical College, make good use of one of the Welsh Hills Lemonade vehicles. (Postcard publisher unidentified)

The biggest annual Catholic event in Cardiff, until the 1990s, was the Corpus Christi – Body of Christ – Celebrations, which first took place in the castle grounds in 1874. (Paviour Cardiff)

When the first
Corpus-Christi
celebrations took
place, the 3rd
Marquis of Bute
was one of the
canopy bearers.
This card is from
around 1911.
(Paviour Cardiff)

Cardiff school
children
head the
Corpus Christi
celebrations'
parade in the
castle grounds.
This card is from
around 1911.
(Paviour Cardiff)

Residents of
Ludlow Street,
Grangetown,
celebrate VJ Day
1945. (Postcard
publisher
unidentified)

Presentation to the City of Cardiff of a German gun, captured at Loos, by the Welsh Guards, 18 November 1915. (Postcard publisher unidentified)

The 3rd Welsh leaving Cardiff Castle. This postcard, and the previous one, were printed for the Welsh Troops' Postcard Day in aid of the National Fund for Welsh Troops. (Postcard publisher unidentified)

The Lord Mayor of Cardiff with Clara Novello Davies, and her Royal Welsh Ladies Choir, prior to their departure for the Paris Exposition on 16 October 1937. (Oxford Studio, Porthcawl)

Médaille d'honneur presented to Madame Clara Novello Davies on 16 October 1937. (Postcard publisher unidentified)

Crowds gathered in 1910 to watch the *Willows* airship prepare for its record flight to London. (W.H.S. & S. Strand Series, posted 14 August 1915)

HRH Princess Margaret visited Llandaff Cathedral, Cardiff, on 26 February 1958. (*Western Mail*)

Willows II airship in flight over Penylan
Hill in 1910. Houses on both sides of
Penylan Hill were built after this picture
was taken. (M. Petschor)

Ernest Robert Curtis (1907-1992), with
his bride Gwen McJennet. 'Ernie' was the
youngest player, at the time, to take part
in an FA Cup Final, when his team Cardiff
City beat Arsenal 1-0 in 1927. (Postcard
publisher unidentified)

Aviation pioneer Edwin Prosser, right, is seen with his Caudron bi-plane at Ely Racecourse on 20 September 1913. (Ernest T. Bush)

In 1935, King George V and Queen Mary visited Cardiff during their Silver Jubilee year and a temporary archway was built in Kingsway for the celebration. The Rose & Crown pub on the right of the picture, which dated from 1787, was demolished in 1974, despite a campaign to have it listed by the Welsh Office. (Postcard publisher unidentified)

12

Pageant of Wales

In 1909, 175,000 spectators attended the National Pageant of Wales in Sophia Gardens. Held between 26 July and 7 August, the pageant depicted the history of Wales from the first century to Henry VIII's Act of Union. Many notables took part, including the Marchioness of Bute, assuming the character of 'Dame Wales', while around 500 prominent footballers enthusiastically helped to storm Cardiff Castle in the name of Ivor Bach. Reconstructed battles unsurprisingly played a large part of the entertainment. Harry Tudor was once again crowned on the field after the Battle of Bosworth, while Caradoc declared war against the Romans. More peaceably, Dafydd ap Gwilym joined twenty damsels to dance on the Pageant Field. Thousands of Cardiff children took part in the closing ceremony, joining up to form a map of Wales.

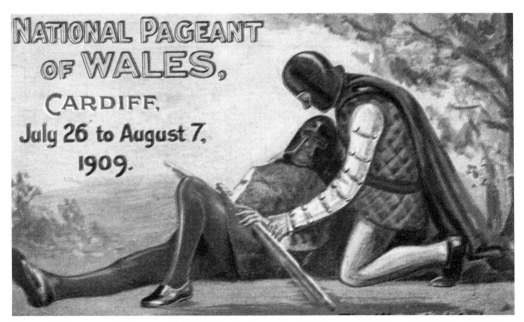

Many of the postcard pictures of the National Pageant of Wales were by Ernest T. Bush and C. Corn of Cardiff. This painted scene of 'The Wounded Archer' is believed to be the work of J.M. Staniforth. (Posted 26 July 1909)

This amazing opening scene, of the ladies in their splendid costumes, was enhanced a hundred-fold when some 700 school girls – in delightful fairy frocks – ran forward from all corners of the field. (Rotary Photo E.C.)

Between 4,000 and 5,000 people took part in the closing scene; at a given signal, the 'fairies' joined hands to form a map of the counties of Wales. This was No. 33 in the series of pageant postcards printed by the publisher. (Rotary Photo E.C.)

13

Royal Infirmary

Following the death of the King in 1910, the South Wales & Monmouthshire Infirmary was renamed King Edward VII Hospital, when a fund was launched to extend the hospital in his memory. Some of the wards were named after wealthy benefactors.

The South Wales and Monmouthshire Infirmary was built at the cost of £23,000 in 1883. It was renamed the King Edward VII Hospital in 1910. (The Strand Series, posted 1922)

The hospital became the Cardiff Royal Infirmary in 1923 and, despite many petitions to keep it open, it closed its doors in 1999. This card is from around 1908. (M.J.R.)

This building was designed by James, Seward & Thomas. The chapel, on the left of the picture, was not built until 1921 and was designed by E.M. Bruce Vaughan. This card is from around 1955. (The R.A. Postcards Ltd, London, EC4)

14

Churches

With the exception of Cardiff Castle, the twelfth-century chapel of St John the Baptist, in the city centre, is the oldest extant building in the capital city of Wales. The historic Llandaff Cathedral has been a place of Christian worship since the sixth century while Trinity Chapel, the first Nonconformist chapel in the town, was built in one of Cardiff's oldest streets – Womanby Street. Cardiff's oldest surviving Catholic church is St Peter's built in 1861, when it was known as St Peter in the Fields.

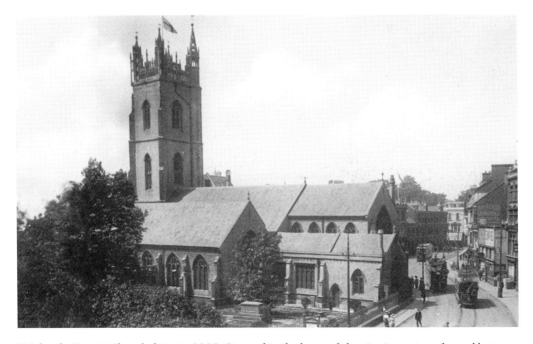

St John the Baptist Church dates to 1180. Situated in the heart of the city, it was transformed between 1453 and 1473 and its magnificent tower was a gift of Lady Anne Neville. This card is from around 1905. (Ernest T. Bush)

The beautiful Llandaff Cathedral dates from 1120, but the cathedral's foundation stone dates back to the sixth century. A landmine brought down the nave of the roof in 1941. This card is from around 1920. (The London Stereoscopic Company Series)

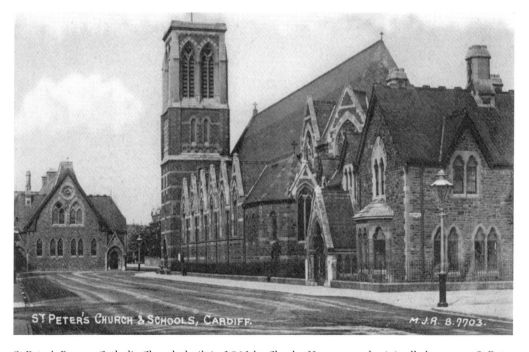

St Peter's Roman Catholic Church; built in 1861 by Charles Hanson, and originally known as St Peter in the Fields, it is Cardiff's oldest surviving Catholic church. A block of flats now stands where St Peter's School, left of the picture, used to be. This card is from around 1920. (Postcard publisher unidentified)

St Mary's Church, Whitchurch; consecrated in 1885, St Mary's Church did not officially become a parish church until 1845, being previously regarded as a daughter church to Llandaff Cathedral. This card is from around 1950. (Postcard publisher unidentified)

St Augustine's parish church in Rumney. The church was originally built from wood and stood for approximately 150 years until it was replaced by a stone construction in 1108. (Ernest T. Bush)

Acknowledgements

First of all, we would like to thank Alun Williams for writing the foreword. We would also like to thank Katrina Coopey and her staff at the Cardiff Central Library Local Studies Department for their assistance.

A special thank you to Richard Barrett for passing on some of his late father's (the great local historian Bill Barrett) picture-postcard collection. To all those people – too many to mention – who offered to loan us their postcards.

To Dennis Morgan and all those other writers, living and dead, whose books we have quoted from. And finally, our grateful thanks to all at The History Press for their help in the editing and production of this book.